Where Plants and Animals Live

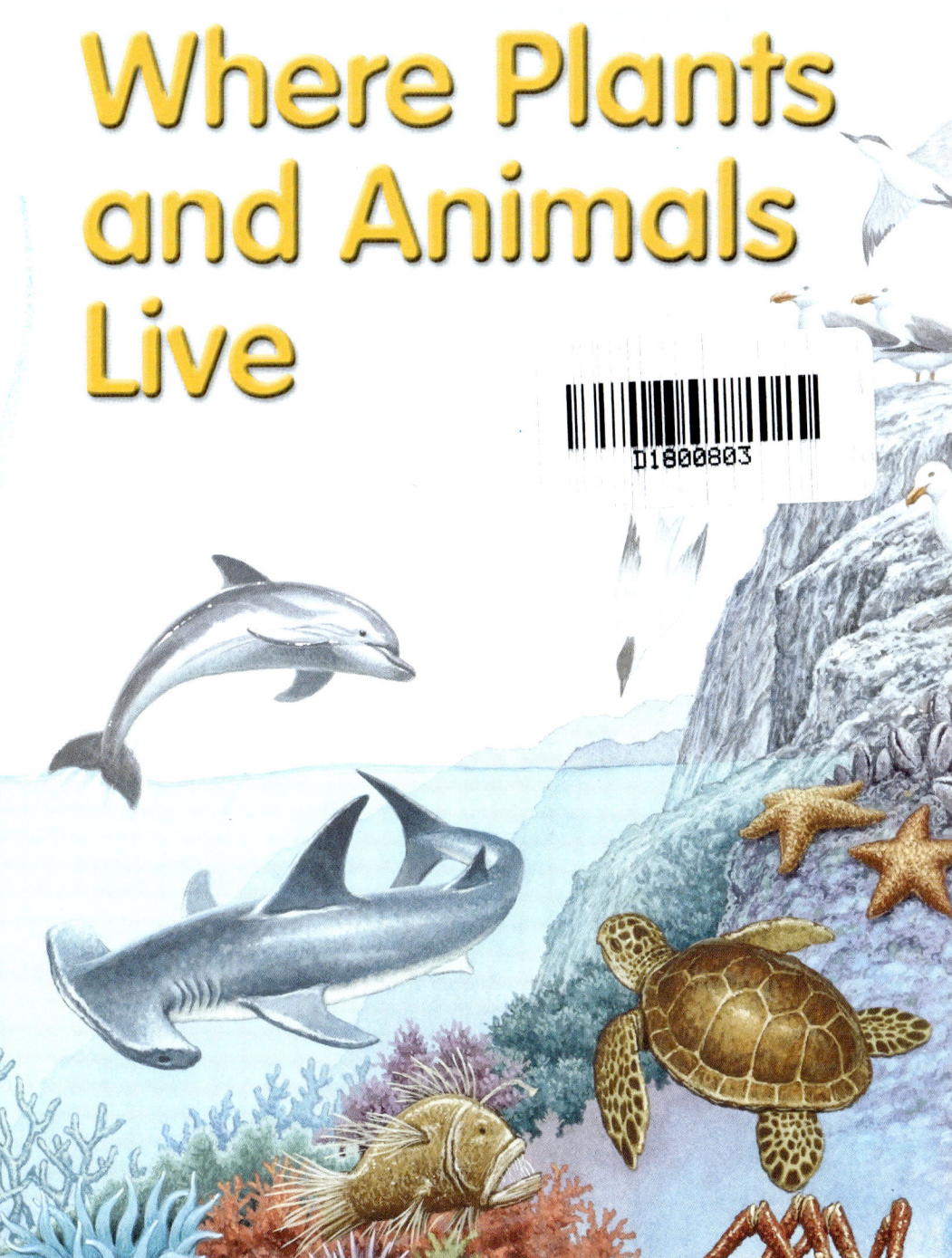

HOUGHTON MIFFLIN   BOSTON

Photography and Illustration Credits
Front Cover Gregory G. Dimijian/Photo Researchers, Inc. **Title Page** Richard Cowdrey. **1** Lynn M. Stone/DRK Photo. **2-3** Richard Cowdrey. **4 (b)** RO-MA Stock/Index Stock. **(tr)** Joe McDonald/DRK Photo. **5 (c)** M. Fogden/Bruce Coleman. **(tr)** Lynn M. Stone/DRK Photo. **6-7** Richard Cowdrey. **8-9** Jim Steinberg/Photo Researchers, Inc. **10-11** Richard Cowdrey. **12-13** Richard Cowdrey. **14** Linda Van Wijk/Masterfile. **15 (t, bm)** Richard Cowdrey. **(tm)** RO-MA Stock/Index Stock. **(b)** Jim Steinberg/Photo Researchers, Inc. **Back Cover** Richard Cowdrey.

Number of Words: 401

Copyright © by Houghton Mifflin Company. All rights reserved.

No part of this work may be reproduced or transmitted in any form or by any means, electronic or mechanical, including photocopying or recording, or by any information storage or retrieval system without the prior written permission of Houghton Mifflin Company unless such copying is expressly permitted by federal copyright law. Address inquiries to School Permissions, Houghton Mifflin Company, 222 Berkeley Street, Boston, MA 02116.

Printed in China

ISBN-13: 978-0-618-75911-8
ISBN-10: 0-618-75911-5

123456789-NPC-12 11 10 09 08 07 06

Contents

1 What Lives in Forests? 2

2 What Lives in Oceans
and Wetlands? 6

3 What Lives in a Desert? 12

Glossary 16

Responding 17

1 What Lives in Forests?

A **forest** is a place
with many trees.
The trees grow close together.
Animals use the living things
in a forest.
Animals use the nonliving things
in a forest, too.
They use these things
for food and shelter.

Other Kinds of Forests

There are many kinds of forests.
Some are hot and wet.
Some are cold and dry.
This forest is cold.

owl

Different kinds of plants live in each forest.
Different kinds of animals live in each forest.
This forest is wet.

parrot

Main Idea

Are all forests the same? Tell why or why not.

2 What Lives in Oceans and Wetlands?

An **ocean** is a large body of salty water.
An ocean is not a living thing.
An ocean has many living things in it.
Some animals live in the ocean.
Some animals live near the ocean.

Ocean animals have special parts.
These parts help them live in water.
Fish have fins and tails to swim.
Fish have gills to breathe.

A Wetland

A **wetland** is land
that is very wet.
There is water in a wetland.
Sometimes the water is salty.
Sometimes the water is not salty.

There is mud in a wetland.
There are plants
in a wetland, too.

There are many kinds of animals in a wetland.
The animals find food and water in the mud, water, and plants.
They find shelter in the mud, water, and plants.

Compare and Contrast

How are oceans different from wetlands?

3 What Lives in a Desert?

A **desert** is a place
with very little water.
It is not easy to live in a desert.
It can be hard to find food.
It can be hard to find water.

lizard

It is hot during the day.
It is cool at night.
Many animals sleep
during the day.
They look for food
at night.

Living in Deserts

Desert plants and animals have special parts.
The parts help them live in dry places.
A cactus has thick stems.
It has waxy skin.
The stems and skin hold water.

cactus

A camel has wide feet.
Its feet help it walk in sand.

Draw Conclusions

Why do many desert animals sleep during the day?

Glossary

desert A place with very little water.

forest A place with many trees that grow close together.

ocean A large body of salty water.

wetland A low area of land that is very wet.

Responding

Think About What You Have Read

1. A large body of salty water is called _____.
   A) a wetland
   B) an ocean
   C) a desert
   D) a forest

2. What helps a cactus hold water?

3. Where do wetland animals find food, water, and shelter?

4. How are all forests alike?